PROGRAMME NOTE

This work draws its inspiration from Australia's so-called IC
northern coastline, Aboriginal and Torres Strait Island cul
Melanesia and Indonesia. *Cello Dreaming* reflects this pluralit,

In one movement, the work is based upon two ideas. The first, heard at the outset, is an adaptation of an indigenous lullaby. The second is a downward-falling melody of the kind known as a tumbling strain. In the central part of the work, the two ideas are brought together, the lullaby here transformed into a more expansive melody. This melody, always played by the cello, also brings the work to its close. In order to create a sense of place, the body of the music is punctuated by references to the sounds of birds, especially those of seagulls, to gamelan-like figures, skin drum patterns and the ruminations of the didjeridu.

Some of the music contains feelings of regret. This is because of my concern about the destruction, mostly through greed and thoughtlessness, of Australia's environment. I would like to think that our northern coastline may long remain an earthly paradise. Indeed, I believe that we are entering a period of greater caring for the fragility of this planet.

PS

Cello Dreaming

PETER SCULTHORPE

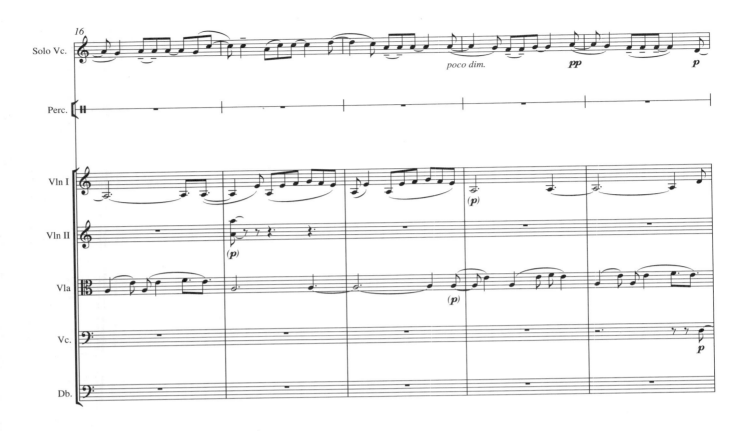

6

* Play seagull-like sounds making glissandi down the G string using the indicated artificial harmonic.
  Retain the same hand spacing throughout the slide so that the glissando keeps repeating the harmonics.

** Quick upward glissandi from any high note. Players should be independent of each other.

8

* Play seagull-like sounds making glissandi down the G string using the indicated artificial harmonic.
Retain the same hand spacing throughout the slide so that the glissando keeps repeating the harmonics.
Players should be independent of each other.

* see footnote on page 6

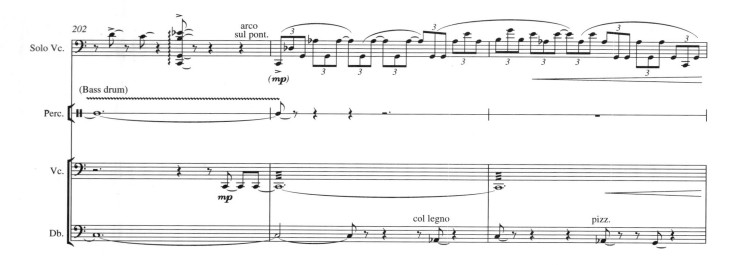

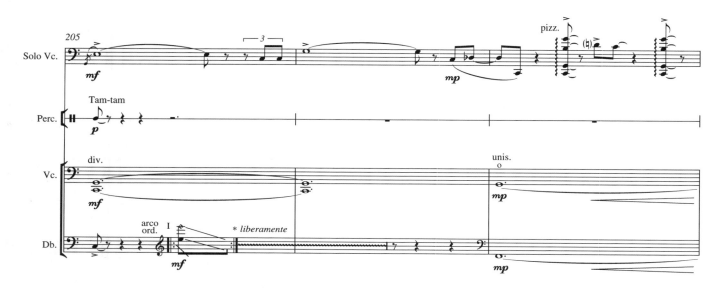

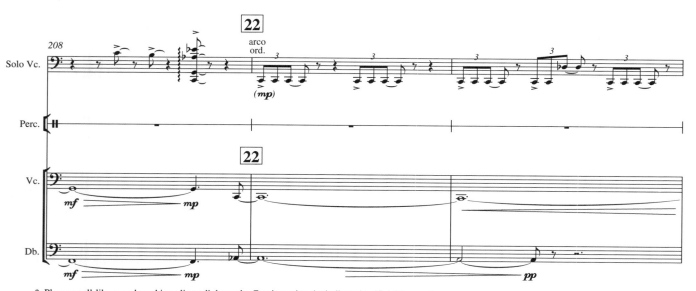

* Play seagull-like sounds making glissandi down the G string using the indicated artificial harmonic.
   Retain the same hand spacing throughout the slide so that the glissando keeps repeating the harmonics.
   Players should be independent of each other.

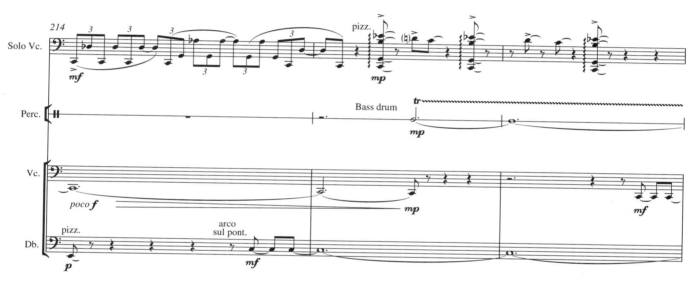

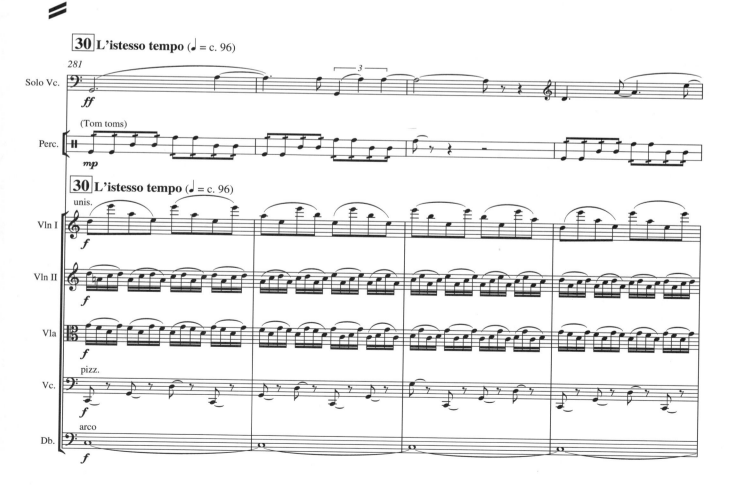

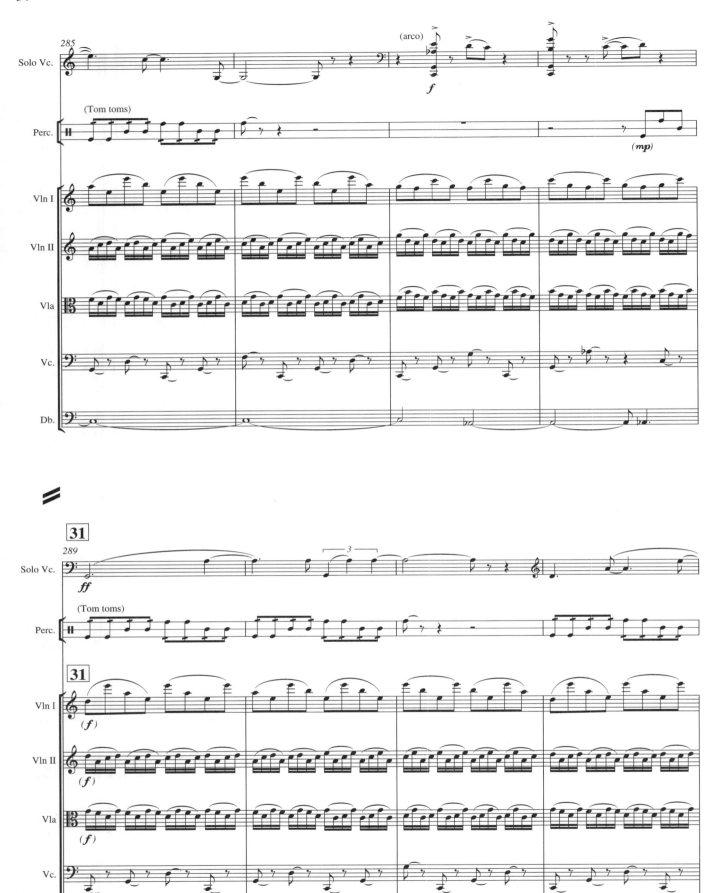

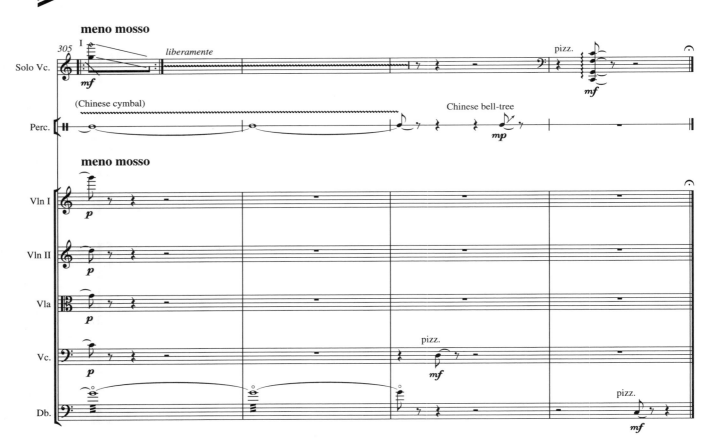

Sydney, March 1998